# bruce springsteen
## 18 TRACKS

Project Manager: Jeannette DeLisa

Art direction: Sandra Choron
Design: Harry Choron
Album cover art: Phil Ceccola
Photography: Debra Rothenberg, David Rose, Pam Springsteen, Phil Ceccola
Jim Marchese, Joel Bernstein, Neal Preston, Annie Leibovitz

WARNER BROS. PUBLICATIONS - THE GLOBAL LEADER IN PRINT
**USA:** 15800 NW 48th Avenue, Miami, FL 33014

WARNER/CHAPPELL MUSIC

Carisch
NUOVA CARISCH

IMP
INTERNATIONAL MUSIC PUBLICATIONS LIMITED

**CANADA:** 40 SHEPPARD AVE. WEST, SUITE 800
TORONTO, ONTARIO, M2N 6K9
**SCANDINAVIA:** P.O. BOX 533, VENDEVAGEN 85 B
S-182 15, DANDERYD, SWEDEN
**AUSTRALIA:** P.O. BOX 353
3 TALAVERA ROAD, NORTH RYDE N.S.W. 2113

**ITALY:** VIA CAMPANIA, 12
20008 S. GIULIANO MILANESE (MI)
ZONA INDUSTRIALE SESTO ULTERIANO
**SPAIN:** MAGALLANES, 25
28015 MADRID
**FRANCE:** 20, RUE DE LA VILLE-L'EVEQUE, 75008 PARIS

**ENGLAND:** GRIFFIN HOUSE,
161 HAMMERSMITH ROAD, LONDON W6 8BS
**GERMANY:** MARSTALLSTR. 8, D-80539 MUNCHEN
**DENMARK:** DANMUSIK, VOGNMAGERGADE 7
DK 1120 KOBENHAVNK

© 2000 WARNER BROS. PUBLICATIONS
All Rights Reserved

Any duplication, adapation or arrangement of the compositions
contained in this collection requires the written consent of the Publisher.
No part of this book may be photocopied or reproduced in any way without permission.
Unauthorized uses are an infringement of the U.S. Copyright Act and are punishable by law.

**d**uring the long intervals between my record releases, as I was spending more and more time in the studio, when I met a fan on the street I was often asked, "What are you guys doing in there?" I regularly pondered that question myself.

What we were doing in there was making a lot of music, a lot more music than I could use at any one time. As a result, my albums became a series of choices—what to include, what to leave out? I based my decisions on my creative point of view at the moment—the subject I was trying to focus on, something musical or emotional I was trying to express. In certain instances, as on *Darkness on the Edge of Town*, *Nebraska*, and *The Ghost of Tom Joad*, these choices crystallized the album I was making. On some of my other records the reasons I had for choosing one song over another, in hindsight, feel a good deal less significant. One of the results of working like this was that a lot of music, including some of my favorite things, remained unreleased.

This collection contains everything from the first notes I sang in a Columbia recording studio, my early and later work with the E Street Band, through my music in the 90s. It's the alternate route to some of the destinations I travelled to on my records, an invitation into the studio on the many nights we spent making music in search of the records we presented to you. I'm glad to finally be able to share this music; here are some of the ones that got away.

Bruce Springsteen
September 1998

# GROWIN' UP

Words and Music by
BRUCE SPRINGSTEEN

© 1972, 1998 BRUCE SPRINGSTEEN (ASCAP)
All Rights Reserved

12

*Verse 2:*
The flag of piracy flew from my mast,
My sails were set wing to wing.
I had a jukebox graduate for a first mate,
She couldn't sail, but she sure could sing.
I pushed B-52 and bombed 'em with the blues
With my gear set stubborn on standing.
We broke all the rules and I strafed my old high school,
Never once gave thought to landing.
And I hid in the clouded warmth of the crowd,
When they said, "Come down!" I threw up.
Oo, growin' up.
*(To Instrumental Bridge:)*

*Verse 3:*
I took month-long vacations in the stratosphere
And you know it's really hard to hold your breath.
I lost everything I ever loved or feared,
I was the cosmic kid in full costume dress.
Well, my feet, they finally took root in the earth,
But I got me a nice little place in the stars.
And I swear I found the key to the universe
In the engine of an old parked car.
And I hid in the mother breast of the crowd.
When they said, "Pull down," I pulled up.
Oo, growin' up.

# SEASIDE BAR SONG

Words and Music by
BRUCE SPRINGSTEEN

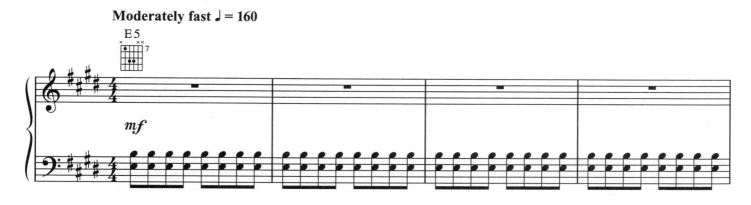

Seaside Bar Song - 10 - 1
0400B

© 1973, 1998 BRUCE SPRINGSTEEN (ASCAP)
All Rights Reserved

Verse 1:

Bil - ly bought a Chev - y, for - ty coupe de - luxe.__ Chrome wheels,__ stick__ shift, give her gas, pop the clutch.__ Lit - tle girls__ on the cor - ner, like a dia - mond they shine.__ Some - day, Bil - ly, I'm gon - na

1. Well,

16

18

20

go on,   go on,   go on.

Oh,_____

ma-ma's gon-na meet you when the morn-ing comes,_____ yeah,

Lyrics: and your Dad-dy's gon-na beat you 'cause he knows you're out on the run. But I don't care._ I wan-na live a life of love_ while the night's still young._____ Al - right____ now.

(Drum fill)

# RENDEZVOUS

Words and Music by
BRUCE SPRINGSTEEN

Moderately ♩ = 126

1.3. I had a dream our love____ would last____ for - ev - er.
2. Have - n't I told you, girl,____ how much____ I like you?

© 1977, 1998 BRUCE SPRINGSTEEN (ASCAP)
All Rights Reserved

# HEARTS OF STONE

Words and Music by
BRUCE SPRINGSTEEN

Slowly ♩ = 66

1. You

*Verse:*

stare in the mir - ror at the lines in your face and you try__ to see,__ girl,__

2.3. *See additional lyrics*

__ the way things were when we were at your place in the days it was

© 1977, 1998 BRUCE SPRINGSTEEN (ASCAP)
All Rights Reserved

'Cause this is the ___ last dance, this is the ___ last chance for hearts of stone.___

2. If there was ___ This is the last

dance, the last chance for hearts of stone.___

**Verse 2:**
If there was something, baby, that I could do,
Something that would last, honey, I would.
But we all know, girl, especially you do
How you can't return to your past, no.
So, girl, close your eyes and I'll be there.
Hold me once more and we can go anywhere.
Ah, we could . . .
*(To Chorus:)*

**Verse 3:**
*(Measures 1-8 Sax solo ad lib.)*
And you cry because things ain't like before.
Well, don't you know they can't be like that anymore.
But don't worry, baby, . . .
*(To Chorus:)*

# WHERE THE BANDS ARE

Words and Music by
BRUCE SPRINGSTEEN

Moderately fast ♩ = 138

Verse:

1. I hear the gui - tars ring - in' out,__ babe, ring - in' out down
2. 3. *See additional lyrics*

Un - ion Street. I hear the lead sing - er shout - in' out,__ girl.

I wan - na be a slave to the beat. Yeah, to - night I wan - na

Where the Bands Are - 7 - 1
0400B

© 1979, 1998 BRUCE SPRINGSTEEN (ASCAP)
All Rights Reserved

Where the Bands Are - 7 - 3
0400B

bands____ are.

(Sax solo ad lib....)

...end solo)   (Guitar solo ad lib....)

bands_____ are,     I wan - na  be  where  the    bands_____ are.

I      wan - na  be,

I      wan - na  be,                I      wan - na

be       where     the      bands_____ are.

*Verse 2:*
I get off from work and I grab something to eat.
I turn the corner and I drive down your street.
Little gray houses, darling, looks like nowhere,
But hey, I know you're hiding in there.
Come on out for just a little while.
You know that heart of stone, girl,
It just ain't your style.
Tonight I wanna feel the beat of the crowd
And when I tell you that I love you,
I wanna have to shout it out loud,
Shout it out loud,
Shout it out loud.
*(To Chorus:)*

*Verse 3:*
I hear the guitars ringin' out again,
Ringin' on down Union Street.
I hear the lead singer shoutin' out and, girl,
I wanna be a slave to the beat.
And I want something that'll break my chains,
Something to break my heart,
Something to shake by brains.
There's a rocker special on tonight,
So meet me on down,
'Neath the neon lights.
*(To Chorus:)*

# LOOSE ENDS

Words and Music by
BRUCE SPRINGSTEEN

out___ on o-pen streets when we had no place to___ go.

2.3. *See additional lyrics*

Loose Ends - 5 - 1
0400B

© 1979, 1998 BRUCE SPRINGSTEEN (ASCAP)
All Rights Reserved

I re - mem - ber how my heart beat when you said, "I love you so." Then lit - tle by lit - tle we choked out all the life that our love could hold. No, no. It was like we held a

*Chorus:*

noose and, ba - by, with - out check, we pulled till it grew tight - er a - round our

42

*Verse 2:*
We didn't count tomorrows,
We took what we could and, baby, we ran.
There was no time for sorrow,
Every place we went I held your hand.
And when the night closed in I was sure
Your kisses told me all I had to know.
But oh, no.
*(To Chorus:)*

*Verse 3:*
Our love has fallen around us
Like we said it never could.
We saw it happen to all the others,
But to us it never would.
Well, how could something so bad, darling,
Come from something that was so good?
I don't know.
*(To Chorus:)*

# I WANNA BE WITH YOU

Words and Music by
BRUCE SPRINGSTEEN

1. Let the

© 1979, 1998 BRUCE SPRINGSTEEN (ASCAP)
All Rights Reserved

be with_ you,_ that's what I wan-na do.__ 2. Now, I I wan-na do.__ Al-right!

(Sax solo ad lib....

...end solo)

48

come when you whis-per, I run when you call.___ When I

see you on the streets___ I fall on my face,___ I

drop to my knees,___ I plead my case.___

Chorus:

Oh,_____ no,___ I wan-na be with___ you, I wan-na

I Wanna Be With You - 8 - 6
0400B

*Chorus:*

*Verse 2:*
Now I lost my job at the Texaco station
'Cause instead of pumping gas I'd dream of you.
I got thrown out of my house,
I got such a bad reputation
'Cause all I wanna do is be seen with you.
They gave me my pay and said walk.
I don't care what they say,
Go ahead, let 'em all talk.

*Chorus 2:*
Till the world falls apart
I wanna be with you,
I wanna be with you.
That's what I wanna do.
Until they will rip out my heart,
I wanna be with you,
I wanna be with you.
Well, that's all I wanna do.
*(To Sax solo Chorus:)*

# BORN IN THE U.S.A.

Words and Music by
BRUCE SPRINGSTEEN

1. Born down in a dead man's town.__ The first kick I took was when I
2.3.4. *See additional lyrics*

© 1982, 1998 BRUCE SPRINGSTEEN (ASCAP)
All Rights Reserved

*Chorus:*

*To Coda* ⊕

1.

54

*Verse 5:*

5. Down in the shad - ow of the pen - i - ten - tia - ry,

out by the gas fires of the re - fin - er - y,

56

Chorus:

Born in the U. S. A. ___ Born in the

U. ___ S. A. Born in the U. S. A.

Repeat ad lib. and fade

Born in the U. ___ S. A.

*Verse 2:*
 I got in a little hometown jam
And so they put a rifle in my hands,
Sent me off to Vietnam
To go and kill the yellow man.
*(To Chorus:)*

*Verse 3:*
Come back home to the refinery.
Hiring man says, "Son, if it was up to me,
I'd go down to see the V.A. man."
He said, "Son, don't you understand?"
*(To Chorus:)*

*Verse 4:*
I had a buddy at Khe Sahn
Fighting off the Viet Cong.
They're still there, he's all gone.
*(To Coda)*

# MY LOVE WILL NOT LET YOU DOWN

Words and Music by
BRUCE SPRINGSTEEN

Bright rock ♩ = 144

My Love Will Not Let You Down - 7 - 1
0400B

© 1982, 1998 BRUCE SPRINGSTEEN (ASCAP)
All Rights Reserved

58

night    I    go_____    to    bed,_____

2.3. *See additional lyrics*

*Verse 2:*
At night I walk the streets looking for romance,
But I always end up stumbling in a half-trance.
I search for connection in some new eyes,
But they're hard for protection from too many dreams passed by.
I see you standing across the room watching me without a sound.
Well, I'm gonna push my way through that crowd,
I'm gonna tear all your walls down.
Tear all your walls down.
*(To Chorus:)*

*Verse 3:*
*(Measures 1-16 Inst. solo ad lib.)*
Well, hold still now, darling, hold still for God's sake.
'Cause I got me a promise I ain't afraid to make.
*(To Chorus:)*

# LION'S DEN

Words and Music by
BRUCE SPRINGSTEEN

© 1982, 1998 BRUCE SPRINGSTEEN (ASCAP)
All Rights Reserved

*Chorus:*

strength of ten.____ So I got a mes - sage for you my friend._____ I'm Dan - iel wait - in' in the li - on's den. Dan - iel wait - in' for that li - on to come. Dan - iel wait - in' in the

68

*Verse 2:*
That old lion's mean and long in the tooth.
And like you, baby, he's out on the loose
Messin' hearts up time and time again.
Well it's time for that messin' to end.
*(To Chorus:)*

*Verse 3:*
At night I hear you out prowling around,
Tearing guys up, scaring 'em down.
Now all that growling's gonna come to no end,
'Cause I'm just biding my time, my little friend.
*(To Chorus:)*

# PINK CADILLAC

Words and Music by
BRUCE SPRINGSTEEN

**Driving blues** ♩ = 120

1. Well, now you___ may think I'm fool - in' for the fool - ish things___ I do.___ You may won -

Pink Cadillac - 5 - 1
0400B

© 1982, 1998 BRUCE SPRINGSTEEN (ASCAP)
All Rights Reserved

*Verse 2:*
Well now, way back in the Bible, temptations always come along.
There's always somebody temptin' you, somebody into doin' something they know is wrong.
Well, they tempt you, man, with silver,
And they tempt you, sir, with gold.
And they tempt you with the pleasures that the flesh does surely hold.
They say Eve tempted Adam with an apple,
But man I ain't going for that,
I know it was her . . .
*(To Chorus:)*

*Verse 3:*
Now, some folks say it's too big, and uses too much gas,
Some folks say its too old, and that it goes too fast.
But my love is better than a Honda, it's bigger than a Subaru.
Hey, man, there's only one thing, and one car that'll do.
Anyway, we don't have to drive it, honey we can park it out in back,
And have a party in your . . .
*(To Chorus:)*

# JANEY DON'T YOU LOSE HEART

Words and Music by
BRUCE SPRINGSTEEN

© 1983, 1998 BRUCE SPRINGSTEEN (ASCAP)
All Rights Reserved

78

Verse 2:
Well, you say you got no new dreams to touch.
You feel like a stranger babe who knows too much.
When you come home late and get undressed.
You lie in bed and feel this emptiness.
Well, listen to me . . .
(To Chorus:)

Verse 3:
Till every river, it runs dry,
Until the sun's torn from the sky.
Till every fear you've felt burst free,
Has gone tumblin' down into the sea.
Listen to me . . .
(To Chorus:)

# SAD EYES

Words and Music by
BRUCE SPRINGSTEEN

© 1990, 1998 BRUCE SPRINGSTEEN (ASCAP)
All Rights Reserved

you're so sure I'll be stand-ing here._____

I guess sad_____

eyes_____ nev-er lie._____

*Repeat ad lib. and fade*

I guess sad_____

*Verse 2:*
Well, for a while I've been watching you steady.
Ain't gonna move 'til you're good and ready.
You show up and then you shy away.
But I know pretty soon you'll be walkin' this way.
*(To Chorus:)*

*Verse 3:*
I know you think you'd never be mine.
Well, that's okay, baby, I don't mind.
That shy smile's sweet, that's a fact.
Go ahead, I don't mind the act.
*(To Coda)*

# PART MAN, PART MONKEY

Words and Music by
BRUCE SPRINGSTEEN

1. They pros - e - cut - ed

Part Man, Part Monkey - 5 - 1
0400B

© 1991, 1998 BRUCE SPRINGSTEEN (ASCAP)
All Rights Reserved

called in that ju - ry and a one, two, three,_ said, "Part man, part mon-key, def -

i - nite - ly."

2. Well, the

Well, the

night is dark,_ the moon is full,_ the flow'rs of ro-mance ex -

Repeat ad lib. and fade

Verse 2:
Well, the church bell rings from the corner steeple,
Man in a monkey suit swears he'll do no evil.
Offers his lover's prayer, but his soul lies
Dark and driftin' and unsatisfied.
Well, hey bartender, tell me whaddaya see?
Part man, part monkey, looks like to me.
(To Bridge:)

Verse 3:
(Guitar solo ad lib.)

Verse 4:
Well, did God make man in a breath of holy fire,
Or did he crawl on up out of the muck and mire?
Well, the man on the street believes what the
Bible tells him so.
Well, you can ask me, mister, because I know.
Tell them soul-suckin' preachers to come on down and see
Part man, part monkey, baby, that's me.

# TROUBLE RIVER

Words and Music by
BRUCE SPRINGSTEEN

Moderately fast ♩ = 132

1. There's a

Verse:
riv - er runs through this val - ley,___ cold___ and deep and
2.3. *See additional lyrics*

Trouble River - 4 - 1
0400B

© 1990, 1999 BRUCE SPRINGSTEEN (ASCAP)
All Rights Reserved

92

Verse 2:
I woke up last night shakin'.
Shakin' from a dream
That all I seen was smiling faces
Staring back at me.
(To Chorus:)

Verse 3:
Snakes crawling in the hi house,
I'm stuck in muddy ground.
Tonight I'm gonna shed this skin
And I'll be breathin' free air now.
(To Chorus:)

# BROTHERS UNDER THE BRIDGE

Words and Music by
BRUCE SPRINGSTEEN

© 1995, 1998 BRUCE SPRINGSTEEN (ASCAP)
All Rights Reserved

95

To Coda ⊕

un - der the bridge.

4. I

*Coda*

Repeat ad lib. and fade

Verse 2:
Campsite's an hour's walk from the nearest road to town.
Up here there's too much brush and canyon
For the CHP choppers to touch down.
Ain't lookin' for nothin', just wanna live.
Me and the brothers under the bridge.

Verse 3:
Come the Santa Ana's, man, that dry brush'll light.
Billy Devon got burned up in his own campfire one winter night.
We buried his body in the white stone high up along the ridge.
Me and the brothers under the bridge.
(To Bridge:)

Verse 4:
I come home in '72.
You were just a beautiful light
In your mama's dark eyes of blue.
I stood down on the tarmac, I was just a kid.
Me and the brothers under the bridge.

Verse 5:
Come Veteran's Day, I sat in the stands in my dress blues.
I held your mother's hand
When they passed with the red, white and blue.
One minute you're right there . . .
Then something slips . . .

# THE FEVER

Words and Music by
BRUCE SPRINGSTEEN

(with pedal)

(Organ enter third time, solo ad lib.)

The Fever - 9 - 1
0400B

© 1973, 1999 BRUCE SPRINGSTEEN (ASCAP)
All Rights Reserved

104

The Fever - 9 - 6
0400B

# THE PROMISE

Words and Music by
BRUCE SPRINGSTEEN

1. John-ny works in a fac-to-ry.

Bil-ly works down-town._

The Promise - 9 - 1
0400B

© 1999 BRUCE SPRINGSTEEN (ASCAP)
All Rights Reserved

112

The Promise - 9 - 5
0400B

113

The Promise - 9 - 6
0400B

a - way.

*Verse 3:*
I won big once and I hit the coast,
But somehow I paid the big cost.
Inside I felt like I was carryin' the broken spirits
Of all the other ones who lost.
When the promise is broken, you go on living,
But it steals something from down in your soul.
Like when the truth is spoken and it don't make no difference,
Somethin' in your heart goes cold.
*(To Coda)*